The Unwanted Blessing

The Unwanted Blessing

E. J. STALLINGS

Foreword by Morgan Meis

Afterword by Debbie Blue

RESOURCE *Publications* · Eugene, Oregon

THE UNWANTED BLESSING

Resource Publications
An Imprint of Wipf and Stock Publishers
199 W. 8th Ave., Suite 3
Eugene, OR 97401

www.wipfandstock.com

PAPERBACK ISBN: 978-1-5326-5758-0
HARDCOVER ISBN: 978-1-5326-5759-7
EBOOK ISBN: 978-1-5326-5760-3

Manufactured in the U.S.A.   11/08/18

llustrations on pages. 47, 63; Work by Tyree Guyton from the Internationally acclaimed Heidelberg Project, Detroit MI.

This Book is dedicated to Emily Besch who has been a constant inspiration and support during the writing of this manuscript and my good friends Morgan Meis and Debbie Blue without whose help this would never have been possible.

Contents

Foreword

Most books about grief, I hate to say it, are terrible. They are terrible because they try to make you feel better right away, or they try to tell you what to do to make it better very soon. Even when such self-help-style books are trying to be gentle and understanding and say things like "you need to give yourself time to grieve" they are still telling you what you "need to do." Other books simply can't wait for you to "lean into" your grief. These books are champing at the bit to prove, basically, how wonderful grief can be. In the end, we'll all realize that God, indeed, is good, or the universe, or people, or whatever. Well, sure, God is good. We all know that. But the proposition that God is good is completely irrelevant to the person in the genuine throes of grief. When you are grieving, you don't want to be told any of this stuff. You don't want to be talked at. You want to be seen and understood.

Jim Stallings has written a book about grief that is not really "about" grief, which is why it is so good. It is really a book written in and through grief. So the grief is just there. The feelings are there, the experiences. They come out slowly and sometimes in unexpected ways. The thoughts and feelings get expressed in vignettes and poems and fragments of, I don't know, something we might as well call prayer. But prayer of the honest sort. Prayer that throws up its hands in confusion and frustration and anger, like the Psalms.

This book was written, in short, by a real person experiencing the hardest things that persons can experience on this earth. This is a heartbreaking book and a soul-shaking book written by a man who's been trying to figure out a thing or two and find a way to go on. Because it is a book of truth and not a book of lies, there are no great revelations. There is no answer. Except that there is one small answer. The book itself is an answer, a response to real life from one man with enough courage to tell it like it is with all the ambiguities and doubt and pain left right in there.

I don't know why things go down the way they do. I don't know why we suffer and why life is the way it is. Neither does Jim Stallings. But he has written a beautiful little book. A hard book, a book that can be hard to read. But a book that is good to read and that should be read, at least by people like us, the ones trying to muddle through as best we can without losing ourselves or our hope or our love for one another.

Morgan Meis

Preface

In 2006 and again in 2011, my world was racked and tilted in an irreversible way. The light angle was different and the familiar became a maze of foreign objects in need of rediscovery in the hue of the aftermath. This book is a collection of literary photographs or renderings of this new world. As Richard Rohr has said, "we don't see things as they are, we see them as we are," and I had been fundamentally changed. There is such sacrifice involved whether voluntary or not from the many who surround us in the adjusting of our sight; not that we are the center of the universe or that all that is happening is either for us specifically, because of us, or about us, but because it is the way things are and it seems we find ourselves constantly adjusting our glasses to clear up the scene before us. The writings contained here cover a span of about 10 years with a few dating back perhaps a decade or so before. They are simply a collection of observations of a landscape that although different in some specifics, I suspect in many ways are common to all of us walking the planet.

Blessings on your re-orientation
Jim Stallings

The Prologue

Grief is realizing that what you had is gone.
You can never be what you once were.

If I study music but never make music, or medicine
but never practice it,
if I only read a billboard about a running shoe
but never try one on,
I do not become involved.
I cannot tell anyone what it feels like.
I can only point to the sign
and by my example
start a whole following of sign watchers.
I have no Gospel in myself.

But then
It's safer to be a student
than a doctor.
Doctors sometimes loose a patient
and musicians sometimes play wrong notes.

Grief has a way of moving us from the auditorium seats
to the stage
whether we are ready or not.

So, In writing this
I can do my part in sharing
and only my part.
Not more than it is
or less than it should be.

Why did Jesus weep when Lazarus died?
Jesus walked out of the tomb
resurrected.
Lazarus . . . walked out
right back where he started.
What had he gained?

God's normal plan of life and death
was changed.
The cycle of death and grieving
God's natural order
his plan
for better or worse
like healing
like sickness.

In the end, there will be no more sickness
we won't need it anymore.
But for now
we need sickness
and grieving.
We always have.
Grieving is more central to God's story
than the events that cause the grief.

Perhaps it is God's unwanted blessing.

Entering into grief is about going to where God is absent for a bit
so that we can find him again.

Surveying the Landscape

We do not see things as they are; We see things as we are

—Richard Rohr

Morning

When I woke up
it was dark
Morning isn't supposed to be like this
Where is the sun?
But, I know it's morning
And, here it sits betrayed by my eyes

As the acid of past experience etches clear, cold lines
onto the polished steel plate of what appears to be,
I sit, making prints
stacking cards in the twilight
arranging the walls and installing the roof
and a new perception of the morning frames its memory
with the darkness of now.

Here, the dichotomy between frame and paint clamps its ferrous chains
and I am shackled to what must be
in the dark void of what should be
Isolated from what I thought I knew
without the inclination to arise.

Quiet except for the breathing
mutely retracing the mental Braille of my history over and again
seeking to craft fact through familiarity.
And, in the long ensuing stillness
a ticking
a waiting
and finally, a stirring
as grey devours black and the chorus of the morning litany
begins to invade my window.

I listen and give thanks.
Morning has arrived right on time.
I was simply early.

Choosing to live in the dark

We crave the reality of Peace, Love and Hope
but we choose to remain in the dark when confronted by
what we don't want to see;
the unanswerable "why" in the face of contradictions.
Instead of embracing the dark we choose "the fall"
where we live out of our own understanding.
The problem is, when we think we understand something
we stop thinking and the light begins to fade.
You see even when we stop thinking
we continue creating our world
reinforcing our assumptions into habits
It's what we create when we are not looking that reveals the most about us.

Practicing faith is preparing for a time when things look different
because if we could really see
we would realize that they look different now
we just don't know it yet.

If you are reading this book then you are aware of the changing landscape. And how, somehow, this same old world looks different, smells different and feels different. But, the world is the same.
It's our eyes that have changed.

God's blessings on your painful new sight and comfort for your loss—all we thought we knew, all we were comfortable with is, at times like this, without even our consent, shed like an old skin and we are remade just a little. You are in my prayers my friend.

The tire jack

Why do spare tires and car jacks in compact cars never seem to go back in the right way.

The man who invented the tire jack left us standing on the side of the road with a jack in our hand peering down into a vacant black hole where tidy engineering in the form of a neatly stowed tire tool once resided. The missing part is not the tire or the jack, but the understanding of the engineering that made it all live happily together.

Once upon a time, the things in life fell in line, rolling along at full speed. And the next moment the pieces have been ripped apart and are held loosely in the hands of a staring fool longing for the engineering.

My how the landscape changes hue after a breakdown; once invigorating scenes of the vast American out-of-doors become stark reminders that we are helpless and alone. Treasures born on eight cylinders become burdens to bear on two legs. Smiles fade in the closing darkness, you search the horizon for a point which isn't here. Suddenly, you notice the intricacies of your immediate surroundings.

The arrow

The past is different from the future.
One of the most glaringly obvious features of this new landscape
is *irreversibility*:
heat doesn't flow spontaneously from cold objects to hot,
we can turn eggs into omelets but not omelets into eggs,
ice cubes melt in warm water but glasses of water
don't spontaneously give rise to ice.
We remember the past, but not the future;
we can take actions that affect the future, but not the past
We are all born, then age, then die;
never the other way around.

Like time itself, that rolls on in spite of our best efforts to slow it down
or speed it up,
the distinction between past and future is consistent
throughout the universe;
flowing in one direction only,
like the red exit arrow at the at a train station, pointing from past to
future.

Training wheels of time

God has given us a great gift by fitting us with these training wheels of time; creating for us the opportunities to stop and reflect on the past and to dream and plan a course for tomorrow. He gives us the chance to develop habits and character, to evaluate the process and make course corrections based on progress. Without time, none of this would be possible.

Writing this, I find myself, like some sort of archeologist, excavating the past, picking up the scraps, straining to recall the feeling of phrases and finding only the memories of words. In the end, I am left with just that—isolated phrases, words, memories of ideas and disconnected imagery. The scene becomes cold like a pharisaical theology,
analytical, structured, searching, and impersonal,
rather than warm and fluid, like spirit;
like life;
like God.

I could describe a photograph of a falling leaf captured halfway between the dark branch and the wet ground, but the life of the event would be missing; like trying to retrace the echoing lines of music as they disappear into the recesses of the canyon.

Music, when it is captured, becomes a jagged groove in a flat piece of vinyl; an arrangement of oxide ions on a tape or a set of mathematical points on a hard drive.. Chameleon-like, it changes shape—hiding in plain view—waiting to be discovered—but it is not until it is let loose, that it sings.

So therefore, I will be still, I will wait, I will capture the music of the spirit onto the jagged landscape of the text, hiding it in plain view, for someone else to set free.

I am sitting this morning. The plates and silverware are on the table. The overhead light is on. It's snowing outside and I am wondering what's missing, as Quinn runs laughing, feeding Cheerios to the dog.

Faith

In What?
In who?
In where?
It's all about orientation.
seeing without distractions
rather than giving reality a disguise.
It's not about pretending.

Grief is real.
Sometimes overwhelming
and pain hurts
sometimes a lot.

Faith is the divine perspective of the present
without the burden of hindsight.

Faith journey

People love to spend time preparing for a life of faith. But why read a book about boat travel when we are already out to sea? Open your eyes and see for yourself. But that's not how we do it. We want to get our feet wet before diving completely in. We don't realize that the clock is ticking, the boat has sailed, and we're aboard.

This realizing that we are already, "in route," is disconcerting.
We are not ready. Years flash by in an instant and time itself collides with our future planning.
When we realize there is no rehearsal, we become disoriented.
As kids, we would yell, "Time," stop the game, regroup our thoughts and start over.
But now, we feel like we've been kidnapped and thrown in the trunk of a rusted old Buick, only to wake up in the middle of nowhere, far away from Kansas. Here there is no smell of the salt air.
Just dust in the throat clawing for Water. We are here.

There is no preparing for a faith journey. We can ignore it, change it, check for direction, struggle with it, curse it, learn from it, laugh with it or even love it.
But, if you are breathing, you are already here.
And God is here too.
He is the one who opened the trunk and let us out;
Freed us
to live, to love, to hate, to quarrel
to become entangled and to be disappointed
to need help, to show mercy
to become interested, to be distracted
to succeed and to fail
to struggle
to grieve
to live.

Hammer and nails

The Bible gives many clues about our Heavenly Father.
Like for instance, that he owns the cattle on a thousand hills.
(at times, however, he seems to keep them fenced up
or worse still, puts them in the care of those who appear to be
working contrary to his best interest)

So, is it God,
or what I thought I heard.
For even a house of cards requires some assembly.
So we stand
with the hammer and the planks of our understanding.

And, we labor on;
Nails into wood, Stone stacked on stone,
stucco, steel and concrete.
But, even as the Mortar dries, the bricks fall off
as Ecclesiastes says, "all is vanity."
Still, I am constrained to go, herded into the sluice.
The way is clear, even dictated:
"appointed to die."
And the provisions are enough . . . for his plan.

But then:
We show up to work and the project's been cut from the budget.
The first workers are paid the same as the last.
And even that pay is not quite enough.
Or so it seems

Perhaps the plan is not for a building.
Perhaps it's more of an invitation to a banquet;
A blueprint for being.
Where we are not called to build after all
But to empty ourselves for another.

The Journey

Death had come
many times before
encountered, once removed,
in the museum of the funeral home,
dressed up, powdered over, smoothed out and peaceful,
and I would say, "if you let go and fall, God is there and fear is gone."

But this time, I didn't let go;
I was pitched from the cliff
into a bare white room where one
barely larger than my two hands lay
in my arms breathing her last.
and I began to scream into the abyss.

Granddaughters

I have no more
a single affinity for this place.
My food has turned to dust
and the very water I drink turns dry in my throat.
Blessings seem but sustenance for my exile;
for there is no mortal salve can ease the pain
of longing across the grave.

To hold again those tiny hands
has set my eyes beyond these shores.
beyond the curtain drawn
where none who pass
may come this way again.

And here in the laughing eyes that
look up from my knee
I find my soul's contention
not in fear of the grave or losing the earth;
But in the longing of this heart
To hold two angels near
For my heart is fettered
both sides of the veil.

Dear God Help

  - My Gravity is broken

Prayer

When we are not thanking God for something or
telling Him how much we love and appreciate Him
we are crying out in concern, grief or pain.

We were birthed into this world and through a thing called death
we are birthed into the next.

People talk about being in the womb
a warm safe place without any cares, difficulties or responsibilities
and express a longing to go back,
to escape the trials,
the worries and the cares
of the present.

It's said that in heaven all of our cares are washed away
that there will be no more sorrow
no remembering of former things.
Why long for Egypt when you are not in the desert?

In our mind, the world began the moment we stepped into it.
We know the essentials
gravity works
we need air to breathe,
water to drink,
food to eat
and shelter.
In effect we are *essentially* concerned with life support
to keep the present functioning as long as possible.

Enter Jesus
someone who knows what went before
and what is to come.
He holds knowledge of the birthing process from both sides
at the same time.
A perspective we are not granted.

Enter faith
faith in relying on someone with this knowledge
to steer our path in the present
out of an unknown past into an unknown future.

Enter the Spirit of God
to connect our present in an intangible unexplainable way
with the before,
the after,
and the God that put it all together.

Enter the grace of God
to listen to our prayers
to comfort
to guide
to ease our burden in our present difficulties
and yes to take the time to answer our request
born of struggle and ignorance.

Enter the Love of God
to smile on the children of God and keep them through the process.

But, grief is real
sometimes overwhelming,
and pain hurts
sometimes a lot.

And because we can't see the beginning and the end
Because God is not walking the dictates of our misguided agenda
Because we are busy buying real estate
when we are supposed to be "traveling through"

God seems not to care,
and the process of prayer seems a pair crutches
for our inherent weakness of not being able to stand on our own.

So then prayer,
perhaps, it's but God's way of granting us enough light
for the next step.

Sometimes it's hard to remember
That even my identity
My being
My fate
Is left to God
Rather than to a self-imposed incantation of survival

Hi B-

Thanks for your thoughts and prayers.
They are much appreciated, more than you will know.

There are two words that you mentioned in your note, loss and why, that get so mushed up that they seem to go hand in hand. I am finding that, although the two bump up against one another, each has its own identity.

Loss is a turning of a page . . . normally accompanied by the word how. How can something be completed without . . .? Or, indeed, how do I survive without . . .? It assumes a broken path or a missing ingredient.
In the midst of a loss/how pairing, I know that God will supply the way and the means. He always does. But it requires reorientation. There is a very big hole that is not going to be filled. The how is learning to navigate the new landscape in light of its "I am"; its absolute reality. The how is a prayer for guidance in the face of loss.

Why, is a prayer for understanding; usually in the light of a change of perception. If we encounter an anomaly that runs contrary to our assumptions, we may ask, "why?"; even before we hit the how. The how will follow of necessity. The why causes us to take a long hard look at where we think we are, where we think we are going, and even ask "what is the point?" always looking for motive, for purpose.

The loss is real, a permanent gaping fixture on the landscape. It is not going anywhere. The how will become evident as we proceed. The why reminds me that I am not in control.

Thanks again for being a friend and for being there,

jim

Waffle House

Ok so what is it about Waffle House?

I always thought it would be great to have
your existence defined by a series of dashing adventures and
mountaintop illuminations, or perhaps by jumping
from the shoulders of one success or victory
to the next tallest one in line
ever onward, ever upward.
But this morning I find myself sitting
in the cacophonous solitude of the Waffle House
where there is something settling about being anonymous
and alone in the middle of a flurry of humanity.

Just 2 hours prior, I received a call
that my cousin's son Dustin died in the early dawn
from a heart attack
he was 34 years old,
the divorced father of two children.

As he lived in Texas,
and as his grandparents
(who had arrived last night to take care of my mother for a week)
are presently packing to return to the lone star,
and as my wife,
is now preparing to swap places with the Texas clan,

I find myself in silent prayer amidst the syrup, eggs and hash browns
of this ubiquitous shrine
where the cantor-like call of the waitress
to the short order cook;
"one over easy, two sausage, sunny, smothered, decaf,"
Is answered by the murmuring response
of the faithful in the orange tabled booths
confessing the past days events one to another,
and at the counter where some may be like Dustin

yesterday, dipping bread in the sop for the last time.

It somehow seems more fitting to offer up prayers here
in this upper room of sweat, breathing, cigarettes,
and the smell of food than at the empty alter bathed in stained glass light.
So now I take out my iPhone
to check the liturgy of the day and prepare my own response,
only to learn that my good friend Gerald passed away.
It appears that today's order of worship is inescapably a requiem preceded
by the Eucharist of coffee and eggs. "This is indeed my body," I believe he
would say,
to all of us.

Go in peace my friends.

Sometimes we don't like where we're found when God moves us to a place that's further down the table than where we think we ought to be.

A sense of purpose

It seems that we identify with characters in a story who stumble onto some sense of their own self-worth outside of themselves; like Lucy in *The Lion the Witch and the Wardrobe*, who stumbles into a magic world outside of her own only to discover that she is an important person. She has worth and value. In fact the world needs her to get along.

I, however, do not generally find myself in these situations. Instead, I find myself and my world standing still while creation, people, seasons, and activities swirl around me unhindered.

A signpost of sorts

The Lord comes to those
waiting for deliverance
where stillness bears the burden of waiting;
who bury their faces.

Pause for a moment

cause no evil whatever happens
Be still
We are not abandoned forever.

Remembering prayer

I have been relearning how to pray;
how to navigate the dead ends of a procrastinating God;
continuously reordering my understanding of existence and of God
in light of the the evidence of experience.
I traverse the crime scene of my
life like the widow scouring for the
lost coin,
amassing a hoard of conflicting entries fearing the worst;
and the prints don't seem to match.
I assume reasoning or reasonableness as I continually search for clues.
What we know depends on where we start.
What we infer depends on what we have been taught.

So back to prayer. "Dear God." That's a good start but what comes next?
Is this a letter or more of a conversation long overdue?
But even if my timing is off, I am told that he will not give me
a stone or a viper
instead of bread.

So far so good. But I haven't asked anything yet.
The bible mentions praying for the sick.
The results seem dicey, haphazard at best.
But still I pray, "Lord fix the broken things"
whether they be people, relationships,
objects or cash flow obstructions;
anything that is not functioning up to par.

Solomon prayed for wisdom.
Through the centuries, the lost have prayed for guidance.
The angry have prayed for victories over their enemies,
for killing.
But that doesn't seem right.
Someone asked once, "and who is my neighbor?"
We might well ask, "and which among your creations is my enemy?"
And here, I'm rather inclined to raise the glass of forgiveness.

Today I am not in an adversarial kind of way.
I am reminding myself that God is in charge;
That he is not known for engaging in conversation
or considering the opinions of others,
that he seems to neglect the obvious
and sometimes switches gears,
and, I am left to work things out alone.

So again, back to prayer.
I sometimes feel it's like purchasing from the company store,
where the necessary ingredients are sitting in abundance,
packed onto shelves like canned sardines, and doled out
in "almost enough" portions for a price slightly higher
than you are able to pay,
keeping you indentured ad infinitum.
Almost like God has forgotten.

Sitting here in a room with my dying father and an elusive God,
it occurs to me;
"it is interesting, that God seemed to make frequent appearances to folks
until the invention of the camera." Perhaps the word appearance is histori-
cally misunderstood.

Randomness

I watched the people move through the room today in random patterns.
Random, not in the sense of purposelessness, but random rather in their relationship to the dying,
to each other,
to their proximity in the room,
to time.
and when viewed from above,
tracing the tapestry of their movements,
reveals a pattern of randomness.
Distance
Perspective
Color
Timbre
Tempo
Size
Purpose

Faith is the art of floating

Living in the likeness of the teacher fueled by grace
God loves our being
not our doing.

Followers don't work at it, they cooperate with it
does that include dying?
Is that what Gethsemane is all about?

This is the hardest place to be
cooperating in change

Embracing the cross

Overcoming the world does not mean cheating death
and living here longer
it means cooperating with God in the process
although process denotes a corporate idea
cooperating with God in life and death is very personal
perhaps that's why they call it cheating instead of overcoming
headed in the wrong direction on a bet you cannot win.

What did God say?
Dying is part of his plan?
it's the elephant in the room
we trust him but we don't want to talk about it
because many of our hopes break down
this side of the turnstile, piled up
dropped by countless hands
resigned to what is from what could be.

How do you surrender
how do you give up
to the mystery which will not clear.

Faith is the art of floating between hope and trust
asking and resigning
to the place where one can only pass alone.

Hi Guys—

I am writing to ask for prayer for my oldest Son Emmett. He went in to the Emergency room last night because he could not keep food down and today his wife called to tell us that he has cancer. It's about 10:30 when I am writing this, and I found out about 3:00 this afternoon—so it's all a really new thing—Deb and I are going up to Nashville tomorrow to be with them—they get the Dr.'s report back Friday about what we are up against and what will need to be done. The worship service is covered here for Sunday. But I will probably still be in Nashville or on my way home. I appreciate your prayers and thoughts. I will send an update when I find out what is what. Please feel free to call me if you need anything.

Thanks

Jim

The mystery of prayer and the apprehension (def #2) of faith

Casting seeds of prayer on the wind
knowing that they will bear fruit
somewhere
at some time
is different from betting all your eggs
on a specific result
from a specific seed.

"Lord help my unbelief"
As I pray for a change
A concrete, black and white, high-resolution change
Yet, the apprehension of the tangible eludes me;
bread for the 5000,
the vacant mat of the paralytic,
the empty coffin of the widows son,
the smooth skin of the leper,
the empty tomb of Lazarus.

Here, my faith turns to hope and wishing.
Here faith has actually become a stumbling block
at the point of intent.
Rather than a means to an end,
faith is a giving of my understanding
to the one who holds even this darkness;
Where I am at the end of options, past the point of flexibility
Bereft of the potential to change and adapt
Where I lie, paralyzed, drowning, while circumstances wash over me
trusting that even my disconnection is not outside his grasp.

Airplane

On an airplane things look small, remote, benign;
our world stretching a mere 200 feet from wingtip to wingtip.
The houses, cars and trees in view,
but not yet on our radar,
are of no immediate concern.
The ground and the horizon also have no immediate
application to our present circumstances
except that we want to stay level with the horizon
and as far above the ground as possible.
At times these points of reference are obscured by clouds
or our gaze is distracted by the heavens.
But, wanting to live forever is like
wanting to take up residence in the clouds.
It just isn't possible.
We were created to fly, not walk on vapor.

Why are we enamored with our Babel in the clouds?
Ecclesiastes says that life is a vapor; that we are either dust or dying grass.
So why is it so hard to embrace flying?
God did not confuse the people in Babel because he was angry,
but rather because they were misdirected by their own imaginations,
trying to lay brick and mortar on a foundation of liquid air.
It just isn't right.
It just won't work.
It can't be sustained.
He wants us to fly; to check the horizon and stay above the ground.
unencumbered with either things of the earth
or the immediacy of the horizon.
Both are provided and maintained by the creator.
Neither are under our control, but they provide direction and reference
to keep us from becoming entangled, weighed down, preoccupied,
off course.
At some point, however, we will all come in contact with the ground,
our point of reference,
because all planes must land.

But in the meantime
If he will mount you up with wings as eagles.
Why walk or sit?
We have wings.

First—thanks for all your prayers—they mean so much.

I just heard from Wendy that the doctors found some spots on his liver from the test yesterday and have scheduled an ultrasound and a liver biopsy today. My mother is coming up to our house and we will be all going up together in just a bit. Just wanted to let you all know.

Jim

A summer of growing

There is a time
between a promise and its fulfillment
that men wait.
The seed has been sown.
It is now the summer of growing.
The cross
the sower
the seeds
the healing of the sick
the breaking of the bread
the tearing of the veil
the rending of a heart
do you hear His voice?
If so
listen and be still.

Friday February 19, 2010

I just wanted to give you all an update on Emmett. Today he had a PET scan—the Dr said that they are trying to discover where we are on a scale from best to worst—he said that all of the tests so far tell us that we are on the worst end of the scale—and now we are trying to discover if we are in the range between the best of the worst or the worst of the worst -

Apparently the PET scan indicated that the cancer had not spread to his bones—which is the first good news we have had since this started. So that puts us in the best of the worst section of the scale. We are thanking God for this news because it means that there is a chance to deal with it.

The biopsy came back inconclusive—so they do not know exactly what kind of cancer they are dealing with—determining this of course will determine the course of the treatment. At present he is on anti-nausea medicine and morphine.

God is good in the midst of all. Thank you for all of your prayers. Please continue to pray that the doctors will be able to determine a successful course of treatment.

Blessings on this Sunday's service—you guys are the best.

Jim

Lord,

I want to lift up my boys and our friend Alyson.
Are we looking at her last footsteps on earth
or will you restore her to us yet again?
I see a line and the difference between what we may want
and what must happen eventually.
And I pray for her restoration
Here and now.

Answer our prayers, Lord
and grant us yet a little more time together here.

T-

I am hanging with the sleeping boy this morning while folks take the opportunity to go to worship. Every once in a while he kind of comes to—in a sort of fuzzy pain drug sort of way. But today—especially—this room is full of our father's love and there is no fear for the moment.
God has somehow seemed to blend and mix the pain and fear with His comfort and mercy in a way that changes the landscape—not in a camouflaging-the-bad sort of way—but in a revealing way. It's much more like a cure than a band-aid; something, somehow real and tangible.

This is very much the scriptures come to life. They never paint the good guys as perfect; but rather paint them as how they are. And; somehow how they are, and how God is, seems to fit; like the situation I find myself in now with a God that is indeed bigger than it all.

In the midst of everything, I find myself checking my perception and my perspective; Looking for holes in the fabric or a heading for the compass, at times second guessing everything. I also find myself asking if I am looking at everything through the cover up of a father's denial; sitting in the middle of a big dark with my imagination painting visible phantasms of self-generated hope.
I find instead that when I let go, God is there, the fear is gone for a moment, His mercy is real, and it's OK. Don't ask me what OK is—I don't know what it is—I just know it is.

your friend

Jim

If I think something is not fair or normal, it is usually because I have sustained a loss or am in the midst of a difficulty.

Hi Guys -

Well we met with the oncologist yesterday—She said that there was no cure for this cancer—that they basically manage it with chemo. She talked about having one or two years with the survival rate for 5 years being less than 5%—of course the 5% means that someone does survive past that. So we are taking it one day at a time—which is how we should be living anyways. I am hoping that since he is young and very healthy otherwise, that his personal odds will be a bit higher, or that it makes him a solid player for the 5% group. Yesterday they discovered that his Stent had moved, so they are going to remove it today. They will also, hopefully in the next couple of days, be putting in a port that will be a permanent fixture for the foreseeable future. This will be where he gets all of his meds (chemo) and where they will be drawing blood when needed. It is hoped that he will start his chemo next Wednesday. Thanks for the prayers—we can continue to pray daily for victory in many ways as we walk through this. I hope we are still praying this way in 10 years.

Jim

When my normal life is turned upside down
and God does not seem to be working for me
I begin to question my beliefs.

Perhaps I am expecting a specific activity or outcome
when that's not what he's about.
But at the moment, there is no relief in sight.
My remedy doesn't effect a cure
and I am looking for a rescue
that doesn't seem to be on its way.

Belief?
must be more than just one more opinion or idea.
It's something we stake our lives on.
But, belief to what;
Back to normal?
As I struggle with faith in the midst of circumstances
the concept of *normal* becomes elusive.

Understanding Belief and comprehending normal
is like considering something as not fair;
because fair occurs when I get what I want
or perceive is right.
If things aren't fair or normal,
I have usually sustained a loss
or am in the midst of a difficulty.

I am reminded of an evening in the hospital room with Emmett surrounded by his friends; I am not sure that many of them were living a *normal* life.
There was J-, who brought Emmett a prayer pager to remind him of the many people praying for him. She has been waiting on a Liver transplant for over a year.
Then there was G-, cheated by a "Christian ministry" from which he could not recoup his losses, while the "ministry" continued to reap the benefits of his labors, bountifully.
There was also A-, living with Crohn's disease; who has had parts of his body removed and is daily dependent on his medication for survival.

So in the midst of it all where does your faith find its *normal*?

Obviously it is not a defined set of circumstances.
The circumstance of normal is where you find yourself;
like the day my wife and I held our granddaughter while she died.
But, in the midst of the awfulness,
I wouldn't have wanted to be anywhere else.

Perhaps, normal is a loving, supporting, praying community
of God's people interceding for each other night and day.
after all
God created normal.

T-

Try as I might, I can't recreate the note my computer devoured.
For me writing is like taking a musical snapshot of place, and time;
like capturing an autumn leaf in mid-fall
Or a ray of sunlight in a hospital room
When I write of the moment, at the moment,
the scene is somehow animated
capturing the life; embracing the energy.
There is something to be said about the vantage point of the present
without the burden of hindsight;
like writing from midstream.

In trying to recreate the lost note from Tuesday
I find myself engaged in the analytical task of
creating with the brick and mortar of keystrokes
the timelessness of the moment gone;
a present in the past
a memory
a monument to something that was;
a retelling of history from the other side of the bridge
rather than
passing on the temporal
to the future.

Yesterday's writing is gone
Trying to recapture it
would only be writing a musical review
of a song you will never hear.

I hope this makes sense in a daylight sort of way after a late night of
writing.

Jim

Buttons

At Christmas time, I wonder about Mary's thoughts at the cross. I know I should be thinking about the stable, but somehow my thoughts wander to the earthly end of things. Did she ponder God's wisdom as she began sorting through all of her thoughts and feelings? The stable is cozy. The cross is cold. I am sure she questioned the order of things in her everyday world as she looked for comfort and reason.

Everyone knows that the blue one comes after the brown, and the red follows the green; and even though the yellow one is a bit smaller it still goes in between the dull black and the shiny turquoise. Whenever you arrange buttons on a table, there is an order that must be followed. Some things, of course, are alphabetized; like animals, going from aardvark and armadillo straight through duck and elephant on your way to zebra. And, other things are arranged by height or size; like the line of boys at the prep school in their brilliant blue vests with the gold crest, standing in line, tallest to shortest, in the crisp air of fall term. Other things are grouped by color or likeness; like sorting marbles or separating the trash from the recyclables. But, this type of order results in groups and piles rather than lines of succession. No, buttons to be properly done should be lined up in order. So why would anyone with a lick of sense put the blue one before the brown or pair up the red and the yellow?

In the beginning, as God was creating the animals, the penguins must have thought that God had it all together. Their bodies were perfect for slicing through the cold arctic water and navigating through the shifting passages of floating ice. The world was perfect and they knew it. Then He made a giraffe. And, I am sure that they thought that God was out of his mind because order and rationality had been severely disturbed. Deliberately. But the penguins had forgotten the one great truth of the stage: The lights are not there for us. They belong to the theater. We are just passing through them for a spell.

Jim—

Yesterday it occurred to me that it is hard for me to know how to be around you. Oh, I can put on my professional cap and offer pastoral care but what I thought about was—how I would be kicking and screaming if my Kid was sick like Emmett and how I would have a hard time being around people who were going about their day as if everything was normal when nothing in your world is normal right now. So anyhow just wanted to share that with you!

E-mail me back at the other address.

T-

T-

You are a good friend, thanks so much for being just that. Please continue to pray with me that Emmett's normal will include many more years to come with his wife Wendy and his little boy Quinn.

Have a great rest of the day,

I will see you Sunday,

Jim

Night

Sitting alone in the darkness
he felt the wind blow softly
through the open window
and drape across him
one last time.

Like a thin robe of airy warmth
the chorus of evening voices
rose about him
as the daylight
became a memory.

In quiet expectation
in the stillness of solitude
he crouched on the soft padded feet
of imagination
listening.

The fields
outside his window
ablaze
in the midnight light
of the sun's reflection
off the ancient moon,

and dreaming he walked unencumbered.

Sometimes another voice is all it takes to transform a day.

Hey there my friend

I am sitting here in a hospital room in Nashville listening to the beautiful sound of my son Emmett breathing. A sound which if events stay their course, will soon fade from this world forever. His cancer has progressed to a point where the doctors can do no more. And so we wait.

I just wanted to send you a note and let you know what a blessing your gesture of kindness meant last summer when you guys signed his copy of the darkest night of the year.

That really made his day. At that point he had been battling the disease about 6 months. Now almost a year later our trail has led us here, where the battle is subsiding and the waiting has set in.

I appreciate all of your prayers and thoughts and look forward to seeing you at the Glen this summer; hopefully with some exciting news of an unexpected measure of grace from the Father. But while I was sitting with my sleeping boy, I just wanted to reach out and tell you thanks. Somehow it helps. My prayers are with you for a great tour.

I wish Deb and I could be with you in Atlanta.

Your friend

Jim

June 3, 2011 12:46 PM

Dear Jim,

I don't really think I'm going to manage to find the right words here. But I will try to do so. . .
Thank you for taking the time and energy to encircle us during this time. Our hearts break as we stand with you . . . in your patience, grief, exhaustion, and hope.

We send prayers for strength, wisdom, and, of course, the all encompassing miracle.

Much Love,

K- & L-

Renewed to Invisibility

(A conversation)

The Dying of the Body
is no small thing
How are we being renewed
as our breathing slows?

Does being renewed mean
ignoring the facts to
grab on to a wish?

I speak out of ignorance
black words of attempted understanding
hoping to form shape and coherence
out of something
I know nothing about.

Faith is cruel in the face of complete separation from the answers.

Dad, what will it be like at the end?
he asked
How did Granddad die?

II

(A departing)

The room takes on a flat appearance.
The luster of life is gone from the air.
Colors are drained to hues of grey and black.

Empty

Useless to him now;
the people stand and weep
and softly sing a hymn

Modern clocks don't tick their warning of the closing darkness
so as not to intrude on our façade of safety.

On visiting the cemetery

While visiting the Cemetery today
I found myself perched at the edge of the world
as though disembarking in a foreign country
that brief moment before you step down and assimilate.
or as though waving goodbye to the space near the turnstile
once occupied by a familiar form
now only air and dust, sliced by the wind, scattered by
time—retreating—reforming itself to make room
for another.
That brief moment before you turn and rejoin the flow.

This scattering of stone seems more a point of departure
than a place of rest.
Each marker a memorial to some last footstep placed on earth
before being lifted to the bottom rung of the ladder
heavy boots—light slippers—sandals
cloth and leather
they are not here—they have climbed on

This morning, I am more aware of the profile of their faces
than the contour of the stone
a spectator—unable to participate yet
allowed to glimpse the form of shadows turning in mid stride.
the chomping—stamping—blowing
The jingle of the harness
the creaking of leaf springs
of people moving on—of people stepping up
of people going out.

And as I watch, my impressions change
like the colors of sunset—changing—fading to stars.
the whoosh and call for exotic destinations—the waning shouts
the boarding and the stillness—the settling dust
the dissipating swirl of air
and I am once again in the world

amidst the fading smell of horse dung among the myrtle trees
stepping down,
turning to rejoin the flow.

Once again, Heaven intrudes
and the worlds are locked together for an instant
then our world changes
and Heaven goes on its way

Zechariah 1:8–11

I saw at night, and behold, a man was riding on a red horse, and he was standing among the myrtle trees which were in the ravine, with red, sorrel and white horses behind him. Then I said, "My lord, what are these?" And the angel who was speaking with me said to me, "I will show you what these are." And the man who was standing among the myrtle trees answered and said, "These are those whom the LORD has sent to patrol the earth." So they answered the angel of the LORD who was standing among the myrtle trees and said, "We have patrolled the earth, and behold, all the earth is peaceful and quiet."

A thorn in the flesh is something that rubs the wrong way and may carry with it remorse or at the very least aggravation, intruding where it doesn't belong. It's by nature invasive. It can be a physical ailment beyond our control; something perhaps God, or someone else, has done to us, or a habit, an addiction, or a character trait that runs contrary to our self-image. But in general, a thorn is a bump in the road, which becomes a mountain when it invades a space deep within, at our heart.

When I had cancer in high school, I was uprooted from my routine in northern VA and spent a month or so in a hospital in New York City. Was it fun? No. Did it hurt? Yes, and it was definitely invasive. On the ward at Sloan Kettering, I joined a new community of folks on a similar journey. I made friends . . . and lost friends. But, even in the months of recovery and hobbling around school on crutches, I never thought of it as a thorn in the flesh. There is a saying that we have in my family "it's nothing but a thing." And that was it. It was just how things were, so you grab your crutches daily and move on; no thorn, just life.

It wasn't until years later when my oldest son Emmett died of cancer, that I encountered a debilitating thorn that I could not relegate to the "thing" category. It's still there, and I expect will be, forever. It raises its razor-like barb at the most inopportune and inconvenient times. And, it has pared my life down to the bone.

A thorn such as this has a way of de-stabilizing a house of cards, of rede-fining relationships with people and the creator.
It is never invited.

When it strikes at the heart, it de-saturates the color in a room, reveals the rust on our treasures, and realigns the pecking order of priorities. It also opens doors and reveals the unseen. It always carries a price, a tax.

What you receive from the transaction depends on your willingness to be broken, to submit to the invasion.

My first thorn gave me the opportunity for a son. The second reminded me of an opportunity for life. This is my body, broken for you. . ..

An aggressive peace

An aggressive peace
absorbs all of my energies in
the lag of my resistance
A fantasy of calm
an opiate of ego
projecting desire as fact
obscuring what is.

Absolved of the responsibility
that accompanies action
embracing a façade of peace
it is easier to not do, than to risk.
And, eventually we fall
victims of our own imagination.

Every act of belligerence
to this comforting anesthesia
hides a barb and draws a price.
Forgiveness is not for sissies
and grace is not for the faint of heart.

We pay for every true act of kindness
as we venture beyond this ease of ego
up the sloping rise
to face the fear of our own identity

and realize
we are not victims
but unique creations.

View From the Road

T-

Can we recognize a dead end from a fork in the road?

There will be dead ends to particular pursuits, activities and wishes.
We may cease from putting something right to our way of thinking, or
pursuing a particular result or acquisition.

And, sometimes God may not seem to be working for us because we are
expecting a specific activity or outcome on his part when that's not what
he's about.

Like, when we are looking for a rescue and it isn't readily apparent that
one is on its way. Or when we are constantly besieged by something from
within or without, and we see no relief in sight and no remedy to effect a
cure.

You asked about belief?
It has to be more than just one more opinion or idea,
because God is asking us to stake our lives on a course of action based on
belief.

Perhaps the dead ends are not necessarily an end to the road but are rather
a measure of something lost. Or on the brighter side perhaps they are a
measure of something learned.

Sometimes I think we are not sure what it is that Jesus suggests.
Sometimes I think we know all too well what Jesus is suggesting,
but we have our itinerary set in a different direction.

So perhaps a way of finding direction is belief in seeing the landscape
for what it is
where the path is probably simply lying in absolute plain view.

Thanks for hanging with me,

Jim

Consider a parable of the seeds

Imagine if you will, a community of acorns planted in the ground beneath the sheltering arms of an old oak. But the acorns are underground and cannot see the world or feel the sun. As time marches on, changes begin to occur. Water from a spring thaw leaches down through the soil. The acorns one by one begin to swell and crack and tiny root-like tendrils begin to emerge from the shell and force themselves deeper into the earth and upward toward the warming nether reach of the topsoil. Spring, re-birth, a return of life after a long winter of death.

But, to the acorns themselves, the whole process is quite disturbing and a great cause for alarm. The smooth shell of the newly planted acorns gives way to wrinkles and cracks and the old self begins to fall away; to rot and decay. The new unfamiliar cancerous-like growth is running rampant and seems contagious. Efforts to smooth the skin and repair the breaches are fruitless and short lived at best, as well recognized forms disintegrate into chaos and loss.

Imagine the ensuing prayers, the search for meaning the seeking out of a calling, of purpose. Surely the creator would not make these beautifully shaped well-crafted beings and then leave them to rot and decay. Their whole world order is crumbling around them. Efforts are made to stop the seepage of water and reinforce the coverings of the acorns, anything to maintain the status quo. Because, if God created it, then this way it must stay.

Schools of thought form and the younger ones are instructed to stay away from the seeping moisture. Many even relocate to dryer soil where the aging process is stalled or thwarted for a bit. As the acorns disintegrate, memorials are constructed and stories are enshrined about the heroic few that staved off the ravages of aging longer than the others. Phrases like, "called to those in wetter climates" are heard. Envoys are sent out and lines begin to be drawn between those living in the damper parts of the forest and the enlightened arid dwellers. Initiatives are developed in an attempt to educate the more moist members of society in the ways of the truth. Barriers are erected to keep out the moisture-ridden and many find themselves called to the barrier ministry. Prayers are offered for those less fortunate and an intense search for meaning arises among the society, particularly those of the dryer persuasion.

Completely unaware of the sun, the breeze, and the leafy branches of the free swinging limbs above, they try in vain to build that lasting thing; That thing that will stand the test of time, as a testament to their "Ozymandias-like" proclamation of the order of their universe. And, as they build, they, like the damp-dwellers, die. For as it is written; (It is appointed for all acorns once to die) (He sends the rain on the just and the unjust).

Evidence of new

It's interesting to note that people don't always want others to see
evidence of healing in their life even though
they struggle towards that goal daily
hoping no one notices that they are hurting in the first place;
that they feel incomplete,
hollow.

It's also interesting that healing begins with
an awareness that something is other
than desirable or whole
and, is measured
with small
repeatable
goals
which
become habits
and in turn
define
new.

Scars of our commitment

In the half glow of a hollow waning moon
where airplanes dream of walking
and mice of wings
we lay in the garden of filtered light
where apples fall in soft staccato while we sleep
expressing the law of attraction between bodies

Hear their call to what is
to dispel the fog of hopeless longing
where what is given is not appreciated
and what is not acquired, becomes
a craving obsession

Leave the hoarding to the blind
who dance in shackles
gathering enough spoils
to break the wagon

There's a road nearby
that lies fallow
at the verge of far and near
without signs or lines
that offers a journey
a chance of being

And there
at the squaring of dark and light
the moon paints shadows through the leaves
sharp edged and defined
carving holes and creating patterns
tilting our senses and obscuring the horizon

Here, we would be free
to breathe life by doing
holding on with only a touch

drinking in the darkness
singing outward the light
dancing the rhythm with no music

And standing on
this precipice where up meets down
we will find our perspective
a dizzying vertigo of possibilities
where In spite the fear of the dark
that draws clear the edges of light
we find a comforting abandon

Here in this meeting of this heat and cold
with its smoking cauldron of questions, fears
and the ambiguities of change
lies, the catalyst of being

And at the centre
at the detonation of colors
there's life
where our experiences are
the pen and pigment of history

Jettison the baggage
of the fear of identity
run up a flag to
the wounds of our commitment
the scars of our success

Offer laments
prayers of confession
melodies of contentment
and Points of confusion

We are Changing

A wild God

We expect god to fit in where we are, to be accustomed to our habits, likes,
dislikes and prejudices; in short our understanding of how things are.
And even though we know better, we put off the unpleasant or inevitable.
It's why religion is convenient and God is not.

He never asks to be let in. He is always there and he is not neat or tidy.
We, of course, have our priorities, the things that must be done; things
that keep us from dancing, seeing, and becoming free.
He comes in as an unsettling distraction that causes us to look beyond the
world we have created in our heads, and consider. . . .
He illuminates the things that we know deep down, and makes us want to
hide and make excuses.

We, notice the fissures in the porcelain and the tarnish on the silver.
At once, we realize that we are part of creation itself.
Our inner world is thrown into disarray and
we try to construct the façade that all is well and under our control;
when it never was, never is, and was never meant to be.

It's His creation and He made it that way.
He created life and death and rules them both.

Once you encounter the wild God face to face your eyes are opened
and you are changed forever.

A letter from Lucy

And so it seems there comes a time
when each of us must cross the line
Let love rule
let faith be found
and seek His light on hopeful ground
look up and find a resting place
a father's love
for a childlike faith

The Epilogue

It's said that we are Fearfully and wonderfully made,
but it seems we're not.
We break down.
We leak blood at times like fluid from the busted block of an old Chevy.
Our programming goes haywire and instead of regenerating dead cells
we grow cancers.
And whatever we do,
the death rate remains at a constant 100%
(Except for Enoch and that Elijah guy).

We know that eventually we are headed for the junk yard.
That sooner or later we will not be able to lift a hand
or talk—or breathe.
And yet we fill our days with acquiring,
with getting,
maneuvering like there is no tomorrow.
But there is, for a while.

Lay not up for yourselves treasures on earth the Bible says
where moth and rust corrupt.
Because, moths and rust are part of the plan
like death and taxes.
They are as sure as the day is long.
They are a fact—Not a possibility.
And thieves,
There are always thieves that break in and steal
with a rallying cry for the common good
except there is no trickle down

Consider the Lilies of the field. They may be clothed
but there is nothing in their pockets.
Perhaps that's why we are to lay up our treasures in heaven.
Because, we have no moth and rust resistance
and our lily like clothes have no pockets.

We try hard to ignore the fact
that our watch spring is winding down,
that it's not being rewound,

that we are created to live but designed to die,
that It's not a dichotomy, it's a blueprint
It's in the engineering.

This is my Father's world
where we are caught in a cycle of birth, death and rebirth,
Not an allegory to be observed but reality to be experienced,
All of it.
We are blessed with life—and with death,
and cursed with a perpetual misunderstanding of it all
that we pass on from generation to generation.

When Adam and Eve made their first suit of clothes
out of prickly fig leaves
they had pockets—I'm sure of it.
In a ravenous instant of blinded insight
they grew in wisdom beyond their years
and understood not a single thing.
So they sewed and hid—and like them
we question the love of a father who will not acquiesce
to our contriving to be
like god.

Out of the misguided desires of our heart
we want to walk on water—but in stilettos,
to be fed like the birds—but hoard the extra like thieves,
to breathe the breath of life as fuel for our pursuit of acquisition
and to find ease for our journey.

But perhaps all of our desires are not misguided.
Perhaps at times, some are the faltering first steps
of real love—of compassion,
when we are not as concerned with pockets—as with blessing,
Or with taking—as receiving—As giving.
If we strive for anything
it should be, to be as the birds,
the withering grass and the fading flower.

Ashes to ashes, dust to dust,
father to son, mother to daughter,
The breath of life is ours to be inhaled and exhaled
for a time—Not stored up in barns.
It is said that we cannot take anything with us,
instead,
when we exhale here we inhale there.
No pockets—No leaky blocks
Just flowers and birds.

Afterword

I'm not entirely crazy about it, but the heart of Christian faith is expressed most resoundingly as death and resurrection. I might prefer something that didn't include tragedy—something a bit lighter or even a tad escapist, something without so much passion and suffering. But I stick with it because it feels like the truth to me. In Christianity we get death and resurrection, not the power of positive thinking.

Jim Stallings is a kindly, honest, sometimes even funny, guide who leads us lovingly into the harrowing darkness, shines a flashlight on it, then gestures to a glimmer of light that might help us find our way back out again. Each time I read this book I feel the darkness differently, and I feel less afraid of it.

I first met Jim at the Glen Workshop in Santa Fe New Mexico in 2009, where I was the chaplain. He sat across from me in the cafeteria, leaned forward intently, tucked his long hair behind his ear and started asking questions. He asks a lot of questions. He's not the type of man who barely listens or who feels the need to mansplain. I was struck by his unguarded curiosity. Most of us operate from behind a protective layer—we are careful not to let on how much we don't know, careful not to act like we are hungry. Jim didn't seem to have that layer. He was disarmingly transparent—like he wasn't going to let any polished affectation get in the way of his pressing sense of inquiry. He wanted to get to the bottom of it. Whatever it was. I was happy he wanted to be my friend.

He wrote me later that summer to tell me his father had died. He said "I feel like I have survived a Tsunami - but now, everything looks quite different in its wake. It's like reality's landscape has a new face; still recognizable but somehow not quite the same." I don't think he was necessarily planning on it at the time, but he was starting to write this book.

I saw him next in the fall of 2010 when he and his wife Deb, came from Georgia to Minnesota to check out what we were doing at House of Mercy, my church. By this time his son, Emmett, had been diagnosed with cancer. We talked about music and Emmett and church. He gave my colleague and I wristbands with Emmett's name on them to help us remember to pray. He was hopeful, maybe even cautiously optimistic. Emmett had a lot of people praying for him. He was surrounded by God and loads of love when he died eight months later.

Jim and I shared our writing over the years. I sent him sermons, he sent me poems and prayers and short essays mulling over biblical stories and theology. When I was experiencing my own tsunami, Jim sent me some of the pieces you have just read. He said he would pray for my family. My 13-year-old daughter had been diagnosed with a large growth on her spine. She had made it through the surgery, but we were afraid and shaken. Jim wrote, "I found a short prayer that I had written out to God during the difficult times when I didn't know what else to say. You can probably relate: 'Dear God, Help, my gravity is broken.'"

When you are afraid it helps to have a gracious companion who understands.

Jim brought more pieces of this book to the spiritual writing workshop I facilitated at the Glen in 2014—a couple of poems framing a narrative about the parable of the seeds. It was a sort of theological grappling with a biblical text and a personal grappling with the possibility that something new and green and alive could grow out of pain. It was about acorns. Jim said he wasn't sure what it was he was writing. He told the work-shoppers that it was "the first draft of an idea that needs a concluding paragraph at least." I am grateful that his grief and wandering and his courage to write it down gave birth to this book of poetry.

When I write the prayers of community for my church, I often ask God to change our perspective—to help us see from a different angle. I think that I am aware, when I ask this, that I might be asking for trouble—but I'm certainly not asking for tragedy. Reading these poems, it is clear how grief ineluctably changes a person (if you don't already know). It's disorienting. It's cold and dark. The color in a room is "desaturated." The "irreversibility" weighs. One feels "bereft of the potential to change and adapt." It is nothing anyone would ask for. It is "unwanted" indeed, but what is astonishing (I don't use the word lightly) is that Jim's words help me to glimpse—without one pious platitude, any false piety or manufactured optimism the (unwanted) *blessing*. Where before he oriented himself by looking at the horizon, now he "notices the intricacies of his immediate surroundings. "He is "paralyzed," "drowning," but there are moments he "rejoins the flow."

He sees more, or more clearly, what is in front of him. What he finds is not comfortable, but it is somehow comforting. He becomes present to what is.

I've been around a lot of people whose talk about God, especially in times of tragedy and grief, makes me uneasy. Like "god" is some personal coach buoying people up in the face of life's challenges. Jim's God is not like this. God procrastinates, doesn't engage readily in conversation. He is mysterious. "Religion is convenient," Stallings says, "God is not." And faith is not like climbing or rising,"Faith is the art of floating." "Faith is a giving of my understanding to the one who holds even this darkness." "Grace is not for the faint of heart." Jim says. No kidding. —But I'm grateful he helps me to see grace right up next to catastrophe.

"In the end there won't be any sickness and grief," says Stallings, but "For now we need it." I don't usually believe religious people who say something like this—I suspect they are trying to make sense of something that may be senseless or being somehow dishonest about the chaos they feel. I wonder if they are trying to shield God or their faith system from too much criticism. Like God would not allow this if we didn't need it—something about God's plan for our lives.

But that is not what the author of this book is up to. There is no trace of apologetics or theodicy—no reassuring lies, or comforting myths in this book of poetry; it is a record of honest discovery.

Grieving is central to god's story, Jim says. And it's precisely because he's committed more to observation than the construction of answers that I believe him.

To use a word like "optimism" (optimistic?) would be wrong. "Hopeful" sounds too thin, although I like the word and long for hopefulness. "The truths of our situation are to be discovered, not manufactured," Jim says. He pays close attention. He sees smoking cauldrons, looming precipices, razor-like barbs and out of brokenness; "tiny root like tendrils" begin to emerge.

Though Jim tells us that grief has changed him. What stood out about him in our first encounter remains very much alive in him: his vulnerable, beautiful curiosity. He doesn't stop asking questions. He brings this quality to his grief. As a pastor, I encounter many grieving people. I'm not sure we are all capable of that—or at least it doesn't come readily. I believe these poems can help to guide us into this way of being.

Debbie Blue

Made in the USA
Columbia, SC
09 February 2019